CAMP
FOR
LOVERS

Published by Page Addie Press
Great Britain
Boot Camp For Lovers: Make Love Last Forever.
The Survival Course For Relationships.

Published by Page Addie Press, Great Britain.
A CIP record for this book is available from the British Library
ISBN 978-0-9556509-3-2   paperback

This book is printed on paper suitable for recycling.

BOOT CAMP FOR LOVERS

Make Love Last Forever

The Survival Course For Relationships

Smith&Jones

PAGE ADDIE

Dedicated To
Lovers

Sue & Bruce

Stu & Carol

Steve & Pia

Steve & Larry

Chloe & Israel

Smith & Jones

Brendon & Liz

Daniel & Tiffany

Nico & Katyuskia

Charlie & Belinda

Carole & Laurence

Consuelo & Colin

Gaye & Graham

Roger & Glenda

Erin & Chang

Pete & Kath

Grant & Sally

Cattis & Eric

John & Jane

Pete & Lynn

Trish & Ross

I wish we could go on sleeping together,
like this, to the end of eternity.

- Ezra Pound

In their choice of lovers, partners reveal their essential nature. The type of human being which we prefer reveals the contours of the heart.

-Josè Ortega y Gassett

Love is a renewable resource.

-Smith & Jones

*Great communication creates great
intimacy. The more intimacy ..the greater your sex life.*

-Smith & Jones

Contents

Smith & Jones
Relationship Secrets

The hard work has already been done for you, by a couple of poor bastards who met at university. One was 17 and the other was 21. Let's for arguments sake, call them, *Smith & Jones*.

It was a classic case of love at first sight. They fell in love without really knowing who they had fallen in love with. Within one week they were ecstatically happy living together. Within one month *Jones* had pissed *Smith* off and for that matter *Smith* was starting to piss *Jones* off too. They started feeling like they were walking through a verbal minefield. Over the following months, one wrong word or change in tone of voice, set off explosions of frustration.

No one truly believed this love could last forever.

Statistically, facts were against them. They were too young. They had no savings. They were both students. Yet within five years, they added a siamese cat, a rosella parrot, four goldfish and two children to their relationship.

Today, *Smith & Jones* have been together for 36 years. During that time they figured a lot of things out. And it shows. They look at each other with interest. And when they talk, it's personal and intimate. Other people notice. Last week they received a text message from a young Vietnamese woman they met recently in Hanoi.

Happy Valentines Day.

Admired your love.

Wish when Dave and I

get married we'll

be happy being

together like you

guys.

Yes, *Smith & Jones* are genuinely still in love with themselves and more in love with each other. They have such an obvious, intimate connection between them, people keep asking *Smith & Jones,* what is your secret.

They say blushing, of course physical attraction, passion and intimacy.

Hotsex has a lot to do with it.

But still, that's not all. What *Smith & Jones* figured out is that if you want a relationship to last, you've got to do some hard work, to make it happen.

More than likely you are made for each other. But if you guys are gonna do the distance, loving long term, it won't just happen. It never just happens. You make it happen. That's why you've picked this book up.

Smith & Jones wrote this book while they were living on China Beach; looking out over the Bay of Tonkin; in a breeze of salted air and jasmine; four summers long and through the house breaking typhoons that followed in four winters. Sitting, writing, talking together. Each chapter based on years of living and loving.

Smith & Jones take love relationships seriously. They wrote this book together because they both believe in lasting love and in creative, dynamic, long term relationships. Their deepest wish is that you can work towards a long term relationship with heart felt intimacy. So you can truly say you want to stay...

twogether

f   o   r   e   v   e   r

and yes, truly believe it.

Love Is a
Four Letter Word

Do you remember when you first met you called each other gentle, cute, cuddly, soft, sweet, sickly names like Babe. Nick-names make our relationship feel private. More secret. That's the way it is. Lovers rename each other. But what about those names you call each other now?

There's a saying: In the first year of a relationship, one partner listens to the other. In the second year of a relationship, the other partner listens. In the third year, the neighbors listen to them both and they're hearing a four letter word and it isn't **Love** Now it's mixed up with those other less endearing four letter words built into phrases like,

Have you ever thought to yourself (even once or twice) what the hell am I doing with you? Why don't I pack my bags and get out. My mother was right! There must be some-one better. What did I ever see in you? I must have been out of my mind!

Hear this! There's no place for this kind of thinking in a long term loving relationship. So sooner or later, you'll both have to sort your issues out, because this constant negative attitude just won't work out. How can you even think of loving and living together, forever. When instead of falling more into love each day,

love is
fall
   i
     ng
       a   p   a   r   t
love is
br eak in
       g

     down.

And you know, that unless you can make this work, you'll be back looking for the "perfect" partner again. Yet, the more partners you spend time with, the harder it is to experience love long term. And at this rate, you'll be pushing up white daisies instead of holding long stem red roses in your hands. So make your love life work now! If you don't sort it out, you'll end up leaving a bad relationship or worse staying in one. A s k y o u r s e l f t h i s q u e s t i o n . Is this relationship almost a statistic? Could it become one? Have you both become jaded enough to secretly believe that any long term relationship is too hard to achieve and impossible to obtain?

The g o o d
n e w s is this.

Without problems, there can't be growth in your relationship. What matters about problems is what you do with them. If you don't or won't look at issues, then you are not going anywhere. But you want to go somewhere. Right? So the first step in creating a long term relationship is to get honest with yourself and each other. It's not going to be easy. You know why? As human beings, we have a great capacity to lie, tell half truths and be manipulative. Deception is the enemy. It's the opposite of being open and upfront with each other.

A relationship is not a place to aerate your lies.If you lie to avoid confrontation, keep the peace or to get our own way. Soon your partner won't be able to rely on you. Rather than hiding the grit of reality and putting up a fake false front, be honest. Tell it as it is. Your truth. That way you'll be a clear thinker. A straight thinker. Live authentically and be true to yourself. Say what you're really thinking. If you hide things to protect yourself or to make your partner feel better, then your partner will get the feeling you're not being truthful, and sure enough you're not. Suspicion creates an invisible line between you. And suspicion makes your relationship questionable because, your lover doesn't honestly know where they stand.

Boot Camp For Lovers will try and help you find your truth and make a shift in the direction of soul to soul love. It's about being together and staying together. It works for any adult relationship. It's not gender specific. Of course, every personal relationship is different, but the key principles are the same.

Boot Camp For Lovers is not a fast read. You have to stop and focus on specific issues and talk them through carefully with your partner.

See the examples we give you as wake-up calls. In one week you'll see the benefits of identifying an issue and making changes. It's hard core and challenging.

- Smith

As you read each chapter, you both need to stop and pay attention. Don't be afraid to look at issues you've been avoiding.

- Jones

Now is the time to look at issues that keep re-surfacing, repeating and staying unresolved. These unresolved issues are like thorns in the heart of your relationship. Unless you work them out, they have a way of working in deeper. Unresolved, they take the lightness out of being together. That is why it's essential to take time to focus on issues. While most relationship experts say " ignore small issues and only look at big ones." *Smith & Jones* discovered, that every issue, major or minor has epervescence. These unresolved bubbles of negative energy are stored as memories. Pressure eventually builds up. Problems come to the surface, creating explosive situations. It doesn't need to be this way. You can reverse the slide towards relationship burnout, where stress and bad feelings are a prelude to a broken heart ending. Keep in mind, whatever issues you have right now can be resolved.That's because

Love is a renewable resource.
-Smith & Jones

In *Boot Camp For Lovers,* you'll be taking a closer look at everyday situations that cause stress in relationships. When you look at each chapter, take a moment to identify and make a note of issues that are affecting your relationship. These are the chapters to work on. Just by doing this you'll intensify your interaction together and get your relationship into great shape. Yes,

it feels hard

because you're retraining and refocusing.

You're going to strip down to bare facts. But be clear, the task is not to fix each other, not to change what your partner thinks or believes, but to gain understanding and greater respect for each other. You'll find yourself loving each other's differences.

Put in a few weeks of concentrated effort... and you'll clear relationship minefields and boobytraps. You'll share more personal thoughts, feelings, ideas and future plans. Negative feelings will be replaced with positive ones. Once you define your emotional authenticity, and share your interior life with your lover, you'll experience greater intimacy. Instead of camouflaging feelings to protect yourself, you'll both open up and expose yourselves. This soul bearing is relationship therapy. It allows your feelings to be known and shared. You'll talk together, not at each other.

All it takes is a good workout with honesty and openess. This is what *Boot Camp For Lovers* is all about. All you need to do is follow four basic...

Boot Camp For Lovers Rules.

BOOT CAMP RULES

Rule 1.
Agree to shake things up.

Ask permission of each other to talk honestly and openly about your relationship. Then you can safely discuss isssues you've been avoiding. That's a great start.

Rule 2.
Bring issues out in the open.

There are no psychologists around here. Only you two know which issues you need to resolve to make your relationship work. You may have to admit you're wrong and that isn't easy. What is easy, is to find fault with your partner! No one's perfect and no one should point the finger. You know, you may be the one at fault. Be honest. By being honest, you become more focused. Your discussions and problem solving capabilities as a couple improve dramatically. When this happens, you'll begin to make positive changes and discover new ways to relate to each other. Both verbally and non verbally.

The way you communicate effects the way your relationship is. Talking deeply about feelings equals sharing. If you're not bringing issues out into the open, how can you resolve anything?

Rule 3.
Make each other aware.

When you recognize problems repeating, make each other aware. How do you do this effectively? You can do it by agreeing to say one of the short phrases you'll find in *Boot Camp For Lovers,* such as Acid Rain. P.K. or Spinach. Use the chapter headings in this book or make up your own. You'll find having an agreed phrase quickly alerts both of you to what is happening! As it's happening... again!

These alerts become a relationship

s.e.c.r.e.t.c.o.d.e.

A private language between you. Say the word and you partner instantly knows how they're acting towards you. Hear the word a few times and you'll see what is going on in the relationship, the emotions involved and patterns of behavior towards each other. You get to see the relationship with clarity. You'll see the facets of various emotions, imperfections and flaws. You start re-seeing what is going on in the relationship, what is happening. This allows one or both of you to turn the situation around and reduce emotional casualties. Soon those recurring big bad issues become non-issues. When you fight less…you love more.

Rule 4.
Do a weekly workout.

Each week, decide to work together on one un-resolved issue. When you identify a problem and look closely at it together, you'll start to understand how attitudes, or what someone says or doesn't say, affects the relationship. Concentrate only on that ONE issue for the next SEVEN days.

After one week you may not have resolved the issue completely, but you'll both recognize the pattern and gain a better understanding. By working things out, you improve the mood of the relationship. Almost overnight, the issue that was so bad, disappears.

Remember this, some issues took longer to develop in your relationship, so some problems may take a day or two more to fix. However long it takes, it's worth working on.

When you change the negative side of your relationship to the positive, you get so much more....

more

connected

more

bonded

more

intimate

more

passion

more

twogether.

Move through *Boot Camp For Lovers* and identify issues that are bugging you. Take one issue each week and focus on it and watch the issue go and the

i   n   t   i   m   a   c   y   g   r   o   w

Get ready to work out your relationship.

1
Agree to talk about issues you've been avoiding.

2
Be honest with each other.

3
Make up a secret code between you. A word or phrase to identify each issue.

4
Focus on one issue in your relationship. And work on that one issue for one week.

1

The Bad Patch

Is falling in love and staying in love with the same person possible?

Yes!

But how do you move past days where love is going to pieces and you have no idea why. You're arguing all the time. You feel unloved. You don't feel in sync. You're just not getting on anymore. While this sounds bad it doesn't mean the relationship is over. You're just going through a bad patch.

It's important to remember: relationships are rarely mergers of strengths melding into perfection. What you have in common is your ability to accommodate each other's differences. What makes you fit together is this: your curves and bumps happen to match someone else's bumps and curves. But at times it just doesn't fit. So expect and accept that you're going to have bad patches.

Everyone goes through hard times in relationships. It just means there are some issues that need to be worked out. While this is going on, it is important to keep in mind, that this situation, this moment in time, is not permanent. No matter how impossible it seems.

Spend this uncomfortable time working it out and not *freaking out.* Given time, patience and a desire to stay together. Every issue can be solved or resolved within a relationship. Rather than focusing on the bad patch, make an effort to shift negative energy that is enveloping you as a couple. You can do this by stopping and deciding to do one good thing together. Even if you don't feel like it. It's really important to redirect yourselves in a positive way.

You've got to

add good things.

Good things balance out negativity. This is where the red roses and chocolates do work. So do moonlight and candle light. They help diffuse tense situations. By their nature they soften shadows and harsh lines. Romantic elements add a sensual dimension to difficult times. Make a move. Do something sensual together. That's essential. When you're back to sharing good times again; you'll realize that the bad patch was a necessary adjustment. You didn't walk out the door, you stayed together and worked through it. The bad patch was a good thing because it was just what you needed to strengthen and move the relationship on. There is a difference between a short term relationship and a long term relationship. In short term relationships partners walk out during bad patches. In long term relationships, they don't. As *Smith & Jones* worked out, if you want a relationship to last, you've got to...

make it happen.

The Bad Patch

Commit to stay together.

Do something good together.

Do something good for each other.

Work through the bad patch.

Trust that you can revive your relationship.

2

Chunky Love

You're constantly telling each other...

"That's it"

Farrrk you.

I've had enough. We're finished. It's all over.

"Forget it"

I can find someone else.

If you're saying this. If these are your terms of endearment. Whatever! Reality is, you're having a series of short term relationships within the same relationship.

In love. All out of love. **In** love. **Out** of love. **In. Out.**

What's the point of investing emotional time, if it isn't going anywhere. Emotional continuity is vital for a long term relationship, otherwise, you'll constantly worry the worst case scenario will happen… your partner walks out of your life and slams the door. But if you love each other with emotional consistency, you'll make a deeper commitment emotionally, mentally, physically and spiritually. Commitment is the most essential ingredient. Commitment is the mainstay. It keeps you *twogether*. Commitment to each other, creates true longevity for the relationship.

So stop unlocking the rush of negative thinking… stop playing with the idea you're leaving. Make the decision to definitely go, or definitely stay. But definitely don't make threats.

Instead, do the opposite. Make a pact to stay together. Confirm your commitment to each other. And promise to never threaten each other with leaving. This promise of stability, by its very nature, has a miraculous way of recreating a

lovebond.

So close. So tangible you can feel it.

Create a moment together. Choose a day to start over with a second ceremony. A commitment from one lover to another to stay *twogether*.

Chunky Love

Be emotionally reliable.

Never threaten to leave.

Put your energy into staying together.

Choose a day to start over with a second ceremony.

3

Sleeping With The Enemy

O.K. so you share your most personal thoughts with your partner.

And what happens?

Inside this intimate setting, your partner does a

180°

change in attitude towards you; a snappy answer will do it; it can happen anytime; sometimes at the end of a day whenever personal reserves are low; the air becomes heavy; feelings become confused; dare we say it, even nasty things are said. This is the partner you can't stand. Or understand.

Instead of ignoring their hissy fit, you can't help yourself. You're waiting for the opportunity to step into their place of tension ... you love & hate it when it happens. You retaliate .... now there's hostility.

Sometimes, we often create problems that don't exist, or exaggerate problems that are already there. We turn stepping stones into stumbling blocks. Just because we feel like it.

Arguments separate you from each other. What you believe is the uniqueness of your love, is now questionable. Now when you turn out the light, you're sleeping with the enemy.

When you argue take care. What is said is never forgotten. From inside love, every word that comes out of your mouth during a heated argument is a weapon. You say things that are false for the sting effect of getting back at your partner. You exaggerate everything to get a reaction. This is the worst kind of fighting. It's unfair fighting,

dirtyfighting.

Here the idea is not to air grievances and reach an understanding, but to wound the other person as deeply as possible. This leaves too many scars. If you are not conscious of what you say, your words can hurt your partner badly. And you can't undo or unsay what you've said. Often what is said is untrue and exaggerated purely to inflict emotional pain. And your partner hears you loud and clear.

Later you try to say, I **didn't** really **mean it.** Of course it's not true. I was just being mean. I'm a **b**astard. I'm a b**itch.**

Too late. What's said can't be unsaid. No matter how often you say sorry, there is no easy erasure. Hurtful words turn into rusty arrows, capable of wounding the heart.

When you fire off your mouth with a grand slam attack on someone's character, you loose their trust and respect. Everytime you verbally slam someone you move further away from each other.

Swear you'll never fire off your mouth in an argument again. It's about practicing self-control and respecting yourself and your partner.

Sleeping With The Enemy

Words do kill relationships.

Once you say something, you can't unsay it.

Swear you'll never fire off your mouth again.

4

Inhouse Fighting

You want to remain close, yet sometimes *someone* does not understand your needs and feelings. So they tend to minimize, or trivialize what you say. *Someone* thinks everything is fine. Yet you feel bad. Because when your partner avoids talking things over, you feel emotionally or verbally unheard and frustrated. You start complaining. You complain to flash a focus on what's bothering you, so they can see there is a problem. After all, you both have to admit a problem exists to solve it. Many arguments are started by a partner who is frustrated with not being heard or feels they are not getting enough two-way talk.

Some relationship experts tell you: to improve a relationship, simply get back to doing the little things you used to do when you first met each other. But the sad truth is, if unresolved issues keep resurfacing as arguments, no amount of favorite candy, gliterazzi bauble or love note, will make any real difference. Relationships nourished solely on occasional dinners, won't cut the sugar.

Unreleased feelings act as ammunition for arguments. Yet often, you argue about small issues not related to the latest thing that is upsetting you.

You know how it goes. Initially you may talk yourself out of opening your mouth. You compromise. Shut up. Or walk out of the room. You desperately want to try to overlook issues and again talk yourself out of bringing it up. But the more you hold back, the more you find yourself taking verbal swipes at your partner. And with all this negative tension tightening emotional nerves, you keep waiting for someone to explode. For without resolution there is a constant unnerving uncertainty. An unresolved issue never goes away on its own. It's like a scorpion, loaded with emotional venom, ready to strike at the heart of your relationship.

"*You* Bitch."

"

What did you just call me?

You Bastard!"

Arguments can get ugly and insulting. You may shout

until the early hours of the morning and problems are still not resolved. They seem worse than when you started.

You think shouting is the only way to let someone know how bad you feel. But while you are shouting, you can't figure out the cause of arguments, because the louder you shout the less you think. That's a scientific fact.

Let's say you're passionate people. O.K. And passionate people fight. Right? **Yes Yes Yes**

An argument can be a passionate power house, if you use it to resolve unresolved issues. The fire of a verbal argument burns off your initial hurt, frustrations and unexploded feelings.

Once you lower your voices and both start talking again, things begin to be productive and non-threatening. It's not easy to start talking again. But talking is the path to understanding and mutual forgiveness.

Now here's the really hard thing to do...during an argument both **apologize.** As soon as you do, you stop the ongoing collateral damage that happens when one or both hold resentment and bad feelings. Neither of you should pretend what just happened, didn't happen. You love each other, you can apologize to each other and it really doesn't matter who says sorry first. You're both wrong at times. The instant you both sincerely apologize, your unconditional surrender creates a new beginning. A sincere apology acts like an effective antedote to bad feelings.

An important thing to remember: you've heard the saying, don't go to bed without making up. Well it's true. If you go to sleep angry, unresolved conflict goes into your psyche where it accumulates on a deeper level and stalks your relationship from the shadows. You can't mentally identify it, but you find yourself reacting in volatile ways towards your partner. This can happen months later and you really can't understand where these bad feelings are coming from. That's why it's vital to resolve conflict on the day you argue. So don't go to bed angry.

You'll find, not resolving differences and grievances creates distance between you. This progresses rapidly into a desire to slam the door on your intimate and physical relationship. The idea of sex goes out the bedroom window.

So how do we fix things when bad feelings have shut the relationship down to a point where you'd rather eat dirt than say something nice to each other! It's a verbal faultline. A chasm wide and deep. It's actually quiet simple. It only takes one person to initiate discussions and close the gap between you. If you are no good at making the first move to talk after a volatile argument, then respect the courage it takes for your partner to open the lines of communication.

Talk about whatever is on your mind. Conflicts get resolved by thinking and talking honestly about what is really going on. Once you do, you'll start sharing all your inner thoughts with renewed truthfulness. This disclosure of feelings moves the relationship into deeper love and understanding. So don't be afraid to lay it all out.

Make the most of an argument. Talk it through when you are calmer but still intense. You'll have energy and passion to do it. Use the energy to work it out. A productive fight ends in a resolution in which each person comes to understand the other's point of view.

What makes a relationship work is this. If you clarify feelings and work them out together, you will notice a renewed romantic vibe and sexual connection. Intimacy creates more intimacy. When you talk and feel truly under-stood and accepted, the gates to the heavenly side of your love open again. You trust each other again. The great feelings of love return. You...

fall more
in love

with your lover.

Inhouse Fighting

Get physically close.

Avoid being critical.

Give up the blame game.

Maintain respect for each other.

Try to see each others perspectives.

Resolve whatever issue caused the argument.

5

What Would Love Do?

You know what a pain in the butt you can be. You can be nasty just cause you feel like it. You can be sullen and silent. A right shit. You may justify your response, by passing blame. Then as your partner tries to discuss things with you... you take a hard tough line and become more disagreeable. How can you expect anyone to love you when you're being a right

P.I.T.A

(pain in the arse)

When you have nagging negative feelings that you don't know what to do with. It's easy to be a P.I.T.A. and send bad vibes your partners way. Every negative action causes a negative reaction. This is a common way arguments start. Now chances are you'll both end up dumping emotional trash on each other. So many arguments stink with the compost of unfairness to them.

Whatever the reasons, remember that you trigger each

other in the positive and the negative. You know and they know when they're being unreasonable. This is where love comes in.

When you know your partner is tired or preoccupied or just has a different opinion, be nice! Ask yourself: what would love do now? Then activate some doable thing, some loving action to reconnect. Do whatever spontaneously feels right. Let it come from the heart. You know what they like. You know when to say, let's have a hug! Make a small gesture. Little things count for a lot. Give some **E**motional **R**esusitation without hesitation.

It may be as simple as a **kiss!**

So how does this feel?

mm m mmmmmmmmmmmmaaahhhhhhh
beautifuk
love you t♥ ♥

What Would Love Do?

Act from the heart

Both of you, go out of your way to show love.

Activate some loving action to reconnect.

Kiss and make up.

6

A_{cid} R_{ain}

In unfamiliar situations, people react in different ways. Take one example: one person is loving the feeling of warm tropical rain on their face. Yet, the other partner fears that death from a lightening strike, is a real possibility.

Really? Yes really! Personality affects how

we react in situations. Metaphorical dark clouds for one person is a typhoon for another. Just because you are not afraid or worried, doesn't mean you can ignore your partner's fears.

If you see your partner is stressed in a situation, don't ignore them or say..."Don't worry, everything's O.K."

Guess what?

It's not O.K. Because they're not O.K.

O.K. you are but they're not. Get it? So what? Shouldn't they just get over it?

No!

Let your partner be themselves. Let them think, say and react to situations as they want to. Let your partner feel the fear. Otherwise you're not validating their reactions. Don't criticize your partner when they show strong emotions. If you're critical, they will see you as detached. Worse, you make them feel pathetic, because they're the one voicing problems. Allow worries to be expressed. Take notice. Don't be inclined to switch off.

Personal reactions never fit into neat calculations. One doesn't have to be rational, logical, scientific or objective all the time. When we are not afraid of emotion…emotion does not embarrass us. There are times when you need to help each other out of situations. And it feels good to give **E**motional **R**escue. We all need **E.R.** at times. We all have moments when we need to be rescued, physically, mentally or emotionally. And moments of strength when you can rescue others. When you give your partner support, you keep them from feeling like they're on their own.

It's safe to let feelings run. Emotions are what make us human. As long as they aren't sweeping away the other partner in an emotional flood.

But no one's going to read your mind! When you're upset, instead of saying nothing, acting weird and making them guess... tell them what's worrying you.

Just say

"Acid Rain."

Say what?

A saying like Acid Rain means: I need your support *now*, because, *I'm freaking out here.*

Smith & Jones discovered something significant. By making up simple phrases like Acid Rain, they could use a private code between them, anytime, anywhere. In a word, you create total awareness of your inner feelings to your partner. In public. In private. Your code tells your partner exactly where you're at.

A couple shared their phrase with *Smith & Jones* recently:

MTM

Now, we had no idea what MTM meant, until they explained it. To that couple, it means: you're being Mean To Me. So be nice! A potent signal they both understood completely.

You two can make up a list, or just one or two, of your own sayings. So either of you can say a phrase and change the situation without having to explain absolutely everything.

Acid Rain

Be supportive.

Don't ignore your partner.

Tell your partner what's wrong.

Agree on private signals between you.

7

Monkey Monkey

Primitive body language is basic and can't be controlled or disguised. When you sense a sensual & sexy change in body code, you can't help it, you're genetically wired to jump in.

When you know someone intimately, you are acutely aware of mood changes expressed through eyes, mouth and lips. The way someone looks at you. The body tells you exactly where it's at. Good moods can be deliciously contagious too. You want to share them.

But it's not in your best interest to get involved with a negative mood. Don't jump in if your partner is in a negative mood, because unfortunately it is also contagious. Contagious like flu. If you catch a bad mood then you're both down with it.

You're not an M.D. are you. A **M**ood **D**octor. It's not up to you to change someone's negative mood. It's up to them to sort out their own stuff. Give a person space. They'll sort it out, without you!

So what about those who love languishing in long moods. Long moody episodes create emotional pollution. Unvoiced negative moods get heavy and dark. They create an invisible disturbance around the place. One partner is left guessing why the other is acting like this. And no matter how hard they try to shake the...

happy rattle ...the *mood* is unsmiling.

Which leaves the other one wondering, why? Is it me? Are they mad at me? What have I done? You rewind the days conversations trying to figure out this prevailing moodiness.

Some partners are masters of the long sulk. They make a conscious decision to use a long moody sulk to force an issue. These moods are weapons to get what they want. This can be as material as the latest mobile phone or as physical as sex or emotional as wanting more attention. They withdraw into monosyllables and turn the relationship into a strategy game. It's all so tedious. And they know it! That's the point.

It shows and everyone can see it. You've heard that expression, "She's such a moody person." "He's always packing a sad." Constant moodiness starts to look like your personality trait. No one can satisfy you. You become known as a person with a personality problem. Eventually your partner looses respect and closes off emotionally and physically because you are too difficult to live with.

Partners want more **jazz** in their life. That's why constant moody blues sessions erode the intimate bond necessary for a long term loving relationship. If you're in a regular bad mood, take note. Accept the fact that you do need to discuss what is going on. Instead of spending time sulking, why not just say...

this bothers me!
and
here's why...

Get it sorted out. Then you can spend time together in a mutually harmonious atmosphere. Instead of playing moody blues alone, you can play with each other.

Monkey Monkey

Give each other space.

Talk about how you're feeling.

Don't use moods as a weapon.

8

Wall Of Silence

Partner: That's a great looking island!

Partner: *No response*

Partner: It'd be a great place to go for a vacation, don't you think?

Partner: *Silence*

Partner: Well, what do you think of my butt?

Partner: *No response*

If you don't bother to talk, you become the silent wall. You make your partner feel like a bore and they end up running monologue after monologue. Because you don't react. If you reply from behind a book; don't look up from your laptop; walk into another room while they're talking; or disappear to the corner store only to return two hours later. If you ignore your partner like this, you're building a great wall between you.

Bigger than China.

Through silence or non participation, you are saying a hell of a lot. Your partner interprets your vacant sign as this... what you're doing is more important than what they have to say.

Wrong!

Wrong!

Wrong!

And when they get upset, you tell them to calm down! What causes the problem here? Fear. Although you may not admit it. Sometimes we make a mental note to avoid certain subjects, because, from past experience, they lead to arguments.

Criticism is another reason we find it difficult to talk. No one likes to be criticized. When your partner constantly offers you unasked for advice, they are being obtusely critical of you. You suspect as much and so you say nothing. Which makes you appear remote and disinterested. Silence is a distancing style of behavior. You both need to work this out. Communication goes both ways.

When your partner shares their feelings, listen to what is on their mind. If you don't talk, if you don't listen, the gap between you creates a wall. The silent wall. Not being listened to is like someone ignoring you or not seeing you for who you are. This creates emotional stress. What's more, if you don't listen with interest, it seems like your partner is not important enough to hear. The inability to listen to your partner carries a poignant loss. You never really know the person you are in love with.

You don't realize how damaging this vacuum is to the essential dynamics of a relationship. In the end, neither of you can talk to each other anymore. You forget how to relate because you forgot to talk. If you quit talking, you loose each other. So how can you be in love when you've lost each other? It doesn't have to go this way.

Communication is an art form. Express yourself and be open to the self-expressions of others. When opinions are listened to and seen as valid, you'll both feel you have something interesting or important to say to each other.

Listen up!

Listen with your heart.

Talk from the heart.

W<small>all</small> O<small>f</small> S<small>ilence</small>

Be generous in conversations.

*A good listener makes **a great** lover.*

Use small talk to bring you together.

*Communication **is an art** form. Express yourself.*

.

9

The Machete

Do you find, when your partner asks you a question and as *you're answering,* they cut in with their own answer.

Excuse me!

Why ask me in the first place?

Cutting someone off when someone is trying to answer the question, you've half arse-asked, is a serious disconnection. Your interruption is rude. By not giving someone a chance to answer, you're indicating that your partner's response is not worth listening to. This may seem a small point, but the point is, devilish things are in the smallest details.

Smith & Jones make this one short and to the point. When you ask a question, give your partner a chance to answer. Then listen to the answer from your lover.

Machete

Practice listening more and interrupting less.

Don't cut your partner off when they are talking.

If you ask a question, listen and wait for the answer.

10

Dirty Flirting

Are you wondering what it would be like to be with some-one else? Is the bush greener on the other side. Is the one, two, three, six, seven year itch really true?

Do you secretly wonder if this relationship has been a mistake. What if this person isn't the one? Is there someone else? Are you supposed to be with someone else? Have you made a serious error of judgement?

Sh↓⚥

Thinking that you have made the wrong decision can keep you from appreciating the relationship you're in. You stay rangy, alert and on the lookout. You make serious eye contact with someone else and before you know it…you're dirty flirting, with all its sex, lies and compromise.

Flirting seriously looks like you desire another relationship.

Your energy for your existing relationship drains away on fantasies. Real love turns into a constant mirage which makes you start thinking about having a relationship with someone else. You kill beautiful feelings every time you do it. Your feelings towards your partner and their feelings towards you get diluted. You both start to loose solid reasons for loving, and you start to care less.

So think about long term consequences before you think about having sex with every...........

womanmanmanwoman

who looks your way.

And when you are caught out, it's not good enough to say,

"Ah come on!"

"You're imagining it!"

Flirting blurs the edges of your relationship. It affects the feelings between you on a subconsious level before you realize it. You can't even be imaginatively unfaithful and think you'll get away with it. Flirting imbeds itself between you, damaging trust and intimacy.

Commitment makes up

90%

of love.

If you're not committed in heart, mind and body then you
block your chance of long term love with your partner.
So stop with the flirting and imaginings!

Love the one
you're with.

Dirty Flirting

If you're flirting…then you're hurting.

Stop fantasizing. It'll only screw up your relationship.

Love the one you're with.

11

Amnesia

Does your partner appear to have selective amnesia? You tell them something important and a few days later they say,

"you never told me that!"

They only hear what they want. And they don't remember what you said. This is a communication breakdown. How can you understand your partner, the heart pouring itself out to you, if you half listen to what they are saying and feeling.

Not being able to really talk about deeper thoughts and feelings makes a person feel lonely. Just because you are with someone, you may not be reaching each other and one partner is living emotionally alone.

It's true.

Anyone can be lonely in love.

You can be living with someone, but not really sharing a life because there's a problem with two way communication. The loneliness comes from knowing you can't contact another person's feelings, no matter how hard you try.

Don't wait for your partner to initiate deep talks. If you don't think you're being heard, what can you do? Try rephrasing what you've just said. Effective communication is not just saying things, but having things heard. Keep in mind, physical and emotional bonds are nurtured through attentive, effective communication. Communication is the glue that bonds your relationship together. Without this kind of foreplay, things get really screwed up. So each partner must take responsibility to

get the
listening part right.

Take time out over coffee, put down the magazine, mute the remote. Make space to communicate. Have a dream! Then share it, even if it doesn't match your partners. Think and talk about your future dreams together. It's a chance to open yourself up and allow another to see your ideas, thoughts and emotions. This strengthens and deepens the love between you.

Amnesia

Get communicating.

Be attentive and learn to listen.

Talk about dreams and plans.

Don't wait for your partner to initiate deep talk.

If you think you're not being heard rephrase what you said.

12

Free Riding

I want love,   *Sure thing. Of course.*

I want money,   *Yeah, yeah*

I want a new car,   *Yeah, yeah*

I want you to make me happy,   *Yeah, yeah*

I want good times,   *Yeah, yeah*

Are you the partner constantly making demands? If you are, you're in a one-way relationship. All your way! What's going to happen?

Your needs, all glittering and paparazzi, will never be satisfied. What happens, is that sooner or later, your partner's ability to live with constant demands wears out. The time line can be minutes or decades long. Until one grey day they're convinced this is not love and your partner turns away from you.

Ask yourself... are you a hot or cold person in this relationship? Warm people respond to others. Cold people never act out of spontaneity but out of instinct for self preservation or ultimate gains. It's impossible to be cold and keep a relationship intimate and personal, when you have a self serving agenda. When you are acquisitive, you accumulate things, not love. You're a taker not a giver. Look at yourself and be really truthful...

Is this you?

If you want to be a lover in a long term relationship you've got to dump the I want, I need, more and more attitude. Don't expect them to do it all. It's an unending list: Holidays. Clothing. Cars. Bills. Mortgages. Money. Get real! Life can be tough enough without you adding to it. Don't expect your partner to do all the providing. The more they do for you, the less you look after yourself. In the end, you become a burden and they'll resent your lack of support. You keep making demands and try to justify your reasons. But sooner or later, when you've used them up and exhausted their resources, your partner will wake up and look in the mirror. And then take a long hard look at where you're at.

A balanced relationship has two equal contributors. Be generous and share responsibilities. Contribute your fair share of money, time and energy.

Create a rich and fulfilling life together.

Free Riding

Keep it real.

Don't be a free loader.

Share financial responsibilities.

Don't expect your partner to provide everything.

13

The Leader

All intimate relationships are about energy. Energy shared. Energy taken. Energy given away and power unrecognized.

In the context of a relationship, conversations and body language between partners make a dialogue that determines the balance of power. Often one person in the relationship dominates; by being more determined; by using a stronger more distinctive voice; by having the first and last say. This makes life difficult. Having to negotiate every situation with a power play partner is exhausting. If one person is dominating, they may be equating intimacy with a form of license to be leader. In this case there may as well be only one person in the relationship. The Leader. It's all about them. Themselves.

"But what if
I am the leader.
Gotta problem with that?"

"Well yeeesss!"

Is your pure brilliance the right way to do things? Not necessarily. The leader always thinks they have a faster, better answer to all situations and takes on the responsibility to ensure their brilliant idea is followed through.

The know it all attitude, acting arrogant, negating, or looking for a way to one-up whatever a partner says, can become a habit. One of you having to defend or prove what you say. This is not what should happen in a shared relationship. If this is happening, you'll have one thing going in the relationship.

Big, fat, **ugly** resentment.

Power and control versus emotional withholding. Both are power plays. There are no winners. There are no Generals here; only Lovers who need to share ideas and decide things together without pressure and conflict. You both walk the planet in your own way *and* you're both brilliant. So when your partner explains something to you, try to understand why they feel or think that way.

When you develop qualities of openness and support, you share a developed inner emotional world with your partner. Creating a balanced and equal relationship is far more rewarding than winning.

The Leader

Find out how your partner thinks and feels.

Respect how your partner thinks and feels.

Equality strengthens and does not weaken your partnership.

14

See Red

The back seat driver is back. Right on your back. They've got answers to questions you didn't even ask. Telling you what to do and how to do it. And isn't it amazing…when you are on your own how you manage to be in control, stay in control and survive, without helpful suggestions!

It goes like this: when someone is in control of a situation, let them drive the car, find a car park, book the hotel, choose the wine and complain about the food. Let them finish whatever they are doing without your unasked for verbal assistance.

The way *you* do something is often totally different to how *they* do it. If *you* try and help when *they* didn't ask, *you* signal a lack of belief in *them*.

Interfering while someone is trying to negotiate situations, creates confusion and frustration. The partner who is trying to sort things, doesn't need quips, interjections, or smart answers from you.

The back seat driver scenario (yes, we all do it) is a huge cause of public arguments and embarrassing flare-ups, manifesting crazy dramatic outcomes for ordinary moments, like parking the car and ramming the

 into the

municipal parking meter; on purpose.

"See *look what you made me do* now!" Run interference in public spaces and you'll end up battling for power, looking crazy and entertaining onlookers in the process. Then you drag the steaming battle home, like pugilistic takeaways, to fight it out, hours later. Sound like you guys? It makes doing things together tense and less fun. Pretty soon you start making excuses to leave one or other at home. What can you do *when someones interfering with* you?

Say

"Who's in the drivers seat?"

"Me!"

Who's in the back seat?

"You."

And, if you're the one running interference, take your hands off the controls. Butt out. Resist looking over your partners collarbone. Stop with the comments. It's not helpful. Your partner can do without it. Give them space to do things their way. And look forward to holding hands in public again.

See Red

Give the respect you expect to get.

Don't tell your partner what to do or how to do it.

Let your partner finish what they've started.

*Give each **other** space to figure things out for themselves.*

15

The Cereal Talker

Blah
Blah
Blah
Blah
Blah
Blah If you do all the talking.

If you are telling your partner how it is. From the minute they wake up. Over espresso, over toast, over eggs. Over and over. Till the light goes out. Then you are the one more interested in doing the talking than listening.

107

Some people announce every little thing they are thinking. And talk about everything they're going to do or not do. When their news is switched on all day; you switch off. Right?

Listening to continual information makes it difficult to differentiate verbal chatter from the need to engage in important discussions. A busy mind filled with monkey chatter leaves no space for exchanging meaningful ideas and thoughts. Instead of constantly talking at your partner and expecting them to fulfill all your needs for personal expression, allow each other space and time out. No matter how much you want to be with someone, take time to relax. Look after yourself. It's your M.B.S.

Mind. Body. Soul.

You've got it all. Educate yourself about yourself. When you have balance and equilibrium in your own life, you bring meaningful expression into your relationship. What you discover, is what you share.

Talking about meaningful expression, there's no room for words & dossiers between the sheets. Or mobile phones, turn them off and your partner on. Make your bed a discussion free zone. Keep your bedroom intimate. We're talking about body language only.

The Cereal Talker

Give each other time out.

Look after yourself, mind, body and soul.

Make your bed a discussion and argument free zone.

Keep your bedroom intimate.

Don't announce every little thing you're going to do.

16

Emotional Library

In every relationship you've ever had, including this one…you have experiences, good and bad, which you retain as memory. All of these personal experiences are stored in the vault of yourself. Some days you can find yourself dragging out

old memories.

Some people call it emotional baggage. *Smith & Jones* prefer to call it the Emotional Library. In these relationship archives, every experience, every reflection, every argument, every joke, becomes a catalogue, defined and cross-referenced to other relationships. So when you come face to face with a difficult situation, it's easy to pull down a volume of experiences from another relationship.

It's so easy to overlay your previous responses onto situations now. And it's so wrong. When you filter everything through your catalogue of past experiences, you're not connecting up in a fresh new way as a couple. Like you should be.

New experiences challenge us every day. Which means we are constantly developing and changing as people. And we need to embrace this. Change renews us. In fact, every seven years our bones, muscles and tissues renew themselves. So does our heart. Love is also a renewable resource, but you've got to work at it.

Change is also part of moving on in any relationship. Part of moving on is about leaving things behind. Especially previous lovers. Yet, some people inadvertently or blatantly invite their past lovers back into their lives. By talking them up or down to the new lover, they compare old loves with new loves. And they use social symbols to do it. How strong, how sexy, how rich, how handsome, how beautiful, how talented, how adventurous, they all were. If you have a habit of talking about your previous partners, what are you really doing? Are you subconsciously trying to shape your present partner into the best of your past lovers? Is this what you want? How does your present partner feel about that?

If you're commited to having a long term relationship make a decision to shelve previous relationships. This makes room for a whole new love story. The relationship script is being written all the time. See your partner as they are right now. Don't use the out-of-date defunct stuff. Use the new and funky.

Emotional Library

See your partner as they are right now.

Don't overlay past relationships on this one.

Make a decision to shelve past relationships.

17

We We

When you met, you were attracted to the fascinating whole person who was living life as they knew it.

Then *We* jumped into bed. *We* were so into each other. *We* began to blend ourselves into one homogeneous couple. Now

We think

We eat

We go

We drink

We have

We drive

We do

We like

We're not individuals.

We're *wewe!*

Weak as weasel pee. No individuality.

Wewe?

Yes? What?

Why did this happen *wewe?*

Because we love each other!

Don't we... *wewe?*

Wewe decided...those unusual charming character traits must go. Like that crazy laugh of yours. That turkey laugh is not allowed out of the house.

Well then...neither are those yellow shiny shoes you bought in Hoi An. They should have stayed there!

Yes, *wewe* needed to change things around here.

Like you!

And you!

This pattern of trying to change each other for the better, is one of the worst things you can do in a relationship. You simply forget who you are in relation to each other.

Smith & Jones have proved that a relationship can grow and develop far beyond ordinary possibilities. To make this happen, you need to do two things.

First, be yourself by getting rid of *wewe*. Make a point of maintaining your own quirky habits. The way you do things is unique and part of your identity. A sense of yourself gives you self-esteem. A full quota of self-esteem is impowering. You look forward to the future because you fully accept who you are. You drive your own destiny. And encompass others in your future plans. Including your lover.

When two lovers realize their full potential as individuals, your partnership is double strength. It gives you power together to adapt to any social physical or emotional dynamics in life. As strong individuals you make a formidable team. Ready for any challenges together. Whether it's a new baby, a new job, winning a lottery or loosing your financial empire and starting all over. When you get rid of *wewe,* your relationship has extraordinary potential.

Second, open your eyes and take a closer look at that special individual you fell in love with. Because they are who they are. And you are you. Simple as that. How you look, think, act, or what you say, makes a unique individual. Be who you are. Give your partner room to become more of who they are, not less than themselves. That way, a fruity complexity develops in your relationship.

W e W e

Keep your own quirky habits.

Be more of who you are not less of yourself.

If you must change someone, look in the mirror.

A relationship is two individuals, living in relation to each other.

18

P.K.

Do you like spontaneity? Do you like experiencing completely unexpected things, like bumping into a best friend you haven't seen since high-school, as you both happened to be on the third floor of the MoMa Gallery, at three thirty-five on a Thursday afternoon, looking at the same Matisse painting. And you were just in New York City for one day. What are the odds of that?

Smith & Jones call these
weirdcrazyconnections

P.K.
moments.

Those personal Pre-disposed Kinetic times when the earth seems to rotate on its axis, just for you. Those moments born from a gut feeling to do something, like phoning a friend you suddenly think about. And as soon as they speak, you know

121

in one nanu second the reason you had to call.

But, how hard is it to act on spontaneous feelings, when you have a partner who's always making, yet another helpful, useful, thoughtful, better suggestion. When *Someone*... interferes and suggests alternatives, they may inadvertently stop you making connections. You don't go ahead and do what you felt you needed to do. That split second in time, which reveals something just for you, vanishes. The intuitive and chance nature of your life doesn't happen for you. Rare moments in life get missed when you don't follow up on your intuition.

Let's rewind a moment. Let's say, you have a spontaneous feeling that flashes across your mind. You want to go to the MoMa. And you don't really know why. Then *someone* tries to change your plan. Go along with it and you'd have missed your friend. And you'd never have known it. What do you do? You can let *someone* know you want to follow your intuition,

by saying, Hey! Don't

P.K.

me please.

P.K. is the freedom to respond to your intuition and inner thoughts. Allow P.K. to bring personal spontaneity into your life. That way you can master your own universe and share the discoveries you find when you come back.

P.K.

Respond to intuition.

Let spontaneity into your life.

Allow your partner to follow their intuition.

19

Rubber Glove

As two individuals, you have different abilities, likes and dislikes. You do what you do best. You take domestic roles by informal mutual agreement. At some point, you both agreed, that one person can do some things better or with greater sensitivity or tolerance than the other. Which is fine. You understand job allocation, it makes perfect sense. But how did you get landed with that rubbishy job that everyone hates doing? And that was months ago. At first, the job seemed O.K. But doing tasks by habit turns even an O.K. job into one you resent. Resentment petrifies energy. To keep energy up, keep things

bendy&flexible.

Talk about tasks that drive you up the proverbial wall. Like always cleaning the toilet. If one person scrubs the loo three times a week, that's one hundred and fifty-six times a year! It's time to relieve them.

Agree with your partner to reverse the tasks. Sure things have to be done, but try swapping jobs about. You clean the bathroom; I'll put the trash out; you wash the car; I'll wash the dog; you barbeque; I'll pick up the laundry; you get the idea.

When the rubber glove's on the other hand, you gain instant appreciation for what each person contributes to the practical side of your relationship. So swap household jobs about. In a few weeks you'll notice the energy levels in the relationship improve 100 % when you clear the air and refresh things.

One more scenario for the domestic scene: You're sitting relaxing with your feet up. *One Person's* vacuuming the apartment. It's not how they do it, it's the way they do it. You can see them from your place on the sofa. Very sucky-moto, heading your way. (just to make you feel bad.) The tension rises as you lift your feet up.

Tension in your living space can be avoided if you both agree to "do it with love or don't do it at all." It stops the nagging and guilt. So when you see *One Person* dragging the vacuum cleaner like a dog on a rope, don't feel guilty. Remember they're doing it with love, so relax. *One Person* is not pretending... they love to do it. All you lazy shites are thinking... great! *One Person* loves to do it, so *One Person* can do it all the time. No slackers. Doing it with love is only for people who love their home enviroment and relationship.

Rubber Glove

Exchange responsibilities.

Do it with love or don't do it at all.

20

Spinach

Somewhere in the relationship, you ask your partner, is my

tie straight,

does my hair look o.k?

Are my undies showing through?

Tell me if I have

lipstick on my teeth.

Wait a minute. Your partner is not your oral hygienist, dresser, make-up or make-over artist. If you invite your partner to keep an eye on your physical appearance, they'll develop a seriously bad habit of constantly checking you out. They'll be in your face 24/7 because you asked them to be your personal assistant. It gets into the Bad Aunty Syndrome, smoothing down your hair and shaping your eyebrows with warm saliva. They take care of you too much!

If you slide under their microscope, you are available for observation. You've created a situation. You allow them to become your body critic and before you know it they're making comments like: You're getting a bit fat, just thought you should know; you should grow your fingernails so your stubby fingers look longer. Unless you're a plastic surgeon, don't go there.

Everyone needs to relax and get away with the occasional bad hair day…but if you've put someone on high alert, they think you want to look great all the time.

Don't ask your partner to be your talking mirror. Or your private mime artist; signaling you when you've got lipstick on your teeth, like running their tongue along their teeth in an effort to let you know your teeth are red. Then there's the little finger pointing, the finger that no one else is supposed to see: *You've dropped food, some stuck on your chin, some spinach in your teeth. I can't stand seeing you like this. Green! Green! I'm helping you out here. Don't look at me like you don't know what I'm saying.*

Proof enough, that there have been a few great mime artists in the world and your partner isn't one of them. So take the hint and stop asking your partner to be your minder. Or they'll end up being your body critic.

Spinach

Look out for yourself.

Stop making your partner your body critic.

Remember to pay each other compliments.

21

Zig Zag

"Can I ask you something?"

"Sure."

"Why is your idea better than mine?"

"Because your idea sux." *(Did I say that?)*

"How about I *never* suggest anything to you again!"

"Fine. Good Idea."

slam!

"Maybe your idea was o.k. after all."

When you met you were total strangers. Then you got to know each other intimately. Now you can see the outline of each other's smile with your eyes closed. When you know someone intimately, you're in sync. You seem to know what the other is going to say, before they've said it. You find yourselves finishing each others sentences. At times it's seamless, as if you've got the same heart beat. It's a beautiful thing.

Then one partner starts to think their way is better. They like to re-vamp your ideas. When you suggest an idea, they put forward another. No matter what you suggest, they have another suggestion, until you can't be bothered thinking about it. If *someone* always has the last say, decisions go one way. The oneness becomes numbness. Flat line thinking. How boring is that.ZZZZZZZZZZZZZZZZZZZZZ

If you don't value what your partner thinks, their energy will go and they'll go cold on you. So when someone has a plan, watch you don't smother it with alternative suggestions. If someone can be bothered to use their own brain to come up with a wonderful bloody idea first ... go with it. This means, if it's red curry at Little India, don't suggest pepperoni pizza at Gino's. Learn to accept other peoples ideas. Try not to adapt, change, or alter it. And next time, when you suggest a flight of fancy first, they'll go along with it.

You don't think or act the same as your partner. That's great. The voyage of the best relationship is a Zig Zag line of a hundred tacks. So why run a straight line through life.

Zig Zag!

Life is incredibly interesting together. Life can be unique, when you make it that way. Remember, the best relationship is a Zig Zag line of a hundred ideas and they're not all yours.

AND how you put forward your idea is important. When you have a thought, don't present it as a question. Should we? Can we? Do you think? How about? What do you think? Forget these continuous ??

When you put forward a good idea as a question, you're asking someone to judge it. So expect to have your idea critiqued and possibly have your mind changed.

To stop *someone* changing the idea you came up with, be more up front. Make a definite point of saying what it is you want to do.

Say

Let's go.

Let's snap the elastic and do it.
(*Or something snappy like that.*)

Zig Zag

Love is a journey. Not a destination.

When your partner has an idea first …go with it.

There are two ways to do something. Your way and their way.

22

Peaches & Pears

What has a can of peaches got to do with you guys? Or a can of plums or pears, or apricots. More than you think! In the Garden of Eden, lovers are talking ad infinitum about fruit... and a whole basket of consumer items in the supermarket.

"Do you prefer curly or straightening shampoo?"

"What! I'm bald... remember?"

"Peppermint or whitening toothpaste or the one with fresh breath stripes."

"No I'm bored with that one."

"What kind of toilet paper do you want Seashells? Stars?"

"No neither. You pay for the patterns. How about plain white?"

"What about recycled? Shit head!"

What say you stop making mutual decisions about thousands of domestic nothings. It doesn't take two massive human brains to make these decisions. It's not domestic physics. It's supermarket shopping! There's nothing sadder than seeing two intelligent people talking about toilet paper at great lengths!

It gets worse. Check out couples doing shopping, one pushing the trolley, one pointing blankly at cans on shelves, trying to get to one mutual mind numbing minor decision on Bartlet pears or Queen peaches. Syrup? Or juice? Sliced? Or whole? And watch the tempo move up to a fruity argument.

Smith & Jones identify this as claustrophobic thinking. Claustrophobic thinking happens when you both do something that doesn't need *twogetherness,* bonded, *en meme temps* (of the same breath) simultaneous, joint decision making. You don't need mutual agreement to buy a tube of toothpaste or a bar of soap. Why not have different toothpastes, two shampoos, in fact, why don't you take two shopping trolleys and start at two different parts of the supermarket. One starts in the fruit department. The other begins with a loaf at the bakery. Go your own way from there.

Go around loading items of your choice. Meet each other halfway and check out each others trolleys. Chuck out cartons, packets, that you've picked up and duplicated. You'll be surprised at how little of these you double-up on.

Shopping your own way gives you freedom of choice. You'll discover you don't actually have to be together to make joint decisions on the small print. You can figure it yourself. Looking at what they've piled into their trolley, you see what your partner loves and hates. You'll learn more about the individual they truly are. Their secret passion for banana custard, baby food, blue corn taco chips, black jelly-beans and green jelly-babies. And they'll soon understand you penchant for Beluga caviar on black rye with a shot of Russian Vodka.

There is only one rule when you shop; your partner must accept what you buy and visa versa.

No returns.
No complaints!

Peaches & Pears

Make individual choices.

Your partner has a right to personal choice. So do you.

23

The Sleeper

Yawn.

Yawn.

Yawn.

Partners get lazy.

They often ask questions like ... what do you want to eat?
What shall we buy? How does this work? Can you fix this?

One partner becomes the sleeper. The other becomes...

the expert.

Like a specialist in the relationship, the expert is always asked about specific things. They become the maitre de, the epicurean authority, the horticulturalist with the green thumb, the mechanic and tyre repair specialist. One partner relies on the other's expertise. While it sounds like a practical idea, *Smith & Jones* believe it turns the relationship into a sleepy backwater.

Now imagine having two individuals in the relationship who both know how things work. You have a more dynamic scenario. You both understand widgets. Organic composting. Four green hands instead of one green thumb. Your ordinary kitchen becomes a souped up kitchen with two great chefs stirring and sautéing different dishes. That's why it's essential to figure things out for yourself.

Do research; gain knowledge and make decisions. Use your own creative juices. Think. Share your ideas. Stimulating the senses makes you more intelligent.

Even if you don't notice a change in I.Q. quota, you'll definitely have a great time admiring each others bonsai and eating each others goulash.

The Sleeper

Extend your abilities.

Break out creative juices.

Make individual decisions.

Stimulate your relationship I.Q.

24

Are You O.K.

In the beginning of your relationship, you talked about so many things and your partner listened. Or you thought they listened. It seemed they understood you. However, later you noticed that when you spoke to them, they often seemed preoccupied and didn't seem to hear you or understand what you said.

Smith & Jones believe that the deepest need in a relationship is for closeness. Intensely intimate relationships have great communication. Sharing part of yourself needs to be mutual and reciprocated to feel accepted and understood.

Intimacy happens between equals. If you don't share, you'll notice that most things you talk about become an issue. When your feelings and actions are misread, you think your partner should know you better. You eventually begin to loose interest in the relationship. When this happens, there is no intimate talk about feelings. And the bottom-line is, no intimacy.

Don't use the idea that "one person can't fill all your needs" to justify a lack of closeness in your relationship.

What can you do here to improve intimacy between you? Simple. Treat each other like lovers and best friends too. Friends are genuinely interested in how you feel. They try hard to find out what is inside.

Friends take turns *talking* and *listening* and *talking* and *listening* and *talking*.

When you speak up and express opinions, friends don't get uncomfortable. They get interested, then make a point of getting involved in the subject, whatever the topic.

So pick up on the subjects your partner initiates. Break the habit of greeting a comment with silence. When they offer their point-of-view let them know it matters. Take what they say seriously. And show it by being supportive. When they forward ideas, be responsive. It works both ways. You validate your partner's opinions and give them personal credibility. And they do the same for you. To find out what your partner thinks and how they are feeling, you need to *take time* out *to ask* the question...

How are you doing?

Make a point to do it often. It's a way of saying I'm interested in what's going on with you. And I care about you.

Share past and present experiences and dreams for the future. When you get to talking in a relaxed open way, like you do with a best friend, eighty-two percent of your relationship problems will be solved (or there abouts). You'll have a great thing going for you, when you share an intellectual and emotional life together. Aim for this.

Enhanced intimacy is where it's at.

Do the intimate talk.

Discuss things that the other doesn't understand. Your relationship is too important to have misunderstandings between you. Exchange thoughts and ideas and immediately you'll feel closer to each other. And there's more to come. The more intimately you relate,

the more intense the passion.

Are You O.K.

Get interested and get involved.

Listen and speak the way a friend does.

Great communication creates great intimacy.

Great intimacy creates great passion.

BOOT CAMP FOR LOVERS

Now you've both read *Boot Camp For Lovers,* you'll have ironed out the emotional fatigues. Issues are no longer camouflaged. You've done the hard yards on your relationship. So now you'll be in great shape for the long term.

Keep it up and carry on loving each other.

69 WAYS

To Stay With Your Lover

1. *Bring issues out into the open.*

2. *Agree to shake things up.*

3. *Make each other aware.*

4. *Do a weekly emotional workout.*

5. *Hurtful words do kill relationships.*

6. *Once you say something, you can't unsay it.*

7. *Love is a renewable resource.*

8. *Trust that you can revive your emotional relationship.*

9. *Commit to stay together.*

10. *Work through the bad patch.*

11. *Don't ruminate and fester bad feelings.*

12. *Do something good together.*

13. Do something good for each other.

14. Keep a sense of humor.

15. Be patient with each other.

16. After an argument use productive techniques to stay close.

17. Maintain respect for each other.

18. Try to see each other's perspective.

19. Avoid being critical.

20. Avoid blaming.

21. Resolve whatever issue caused the fight.

22. Get physically close to help get back good feelings.

23. Activate some doable thing.

24. Don't take your partners negative behavior personally.

25. Avoid catching a negative mood.

26. Turn off negative thoughts.

27. Make sure that each of you feels

better about the other person.

28. Be supportive.

29. Don't ignore your partner.

30. Contribute to a love relationship physically, verbally

and emotionally.

31. *Agree private codes between you.*

32. *Allow each other their personal moods.*

33. *Don't use your mood to manipulate and get your way.*

34. *Communication is an art form.*

35. *Express yourself.*

36. *To understand your partner - listen to what they are saying.*

37. *Equality strengthens and does not weaken your partnership.*

38. *Create a balanced and equal relationship.*

39. *The silent treatment creates emotional stress.*

40. *A good listener makes a great lover.*

41. *Be generous in conversations.*

42. *Practice listening more and interrupting less.*

43. *Small talk brings you together.*

44. *Communication is the emotional glue that holds relationships together.*

45. *To understand your partner... listen to what they're saying.*

46. *If you're flirting...then you're hurting.*

47. *Keep it real.*

48. *Share responsibilities.*

49. *Give the respect you expect to get.*

50. *Talk as equals do.*

51. *Keep your bedroom intimate.*

52. *Make your bedroom a discussion free zone.*

53. *Don't overlay past relationships on this one.*

54. *See your partner as they are right now.*

55. Be more of who you are, not less of yourself.

56. Don't block personal synchronicity by interfering and suggesting alternatives.

57. Be an equal contributor.

58. Stop making your partner your body critic.

59. Pay each other compliments.

60. When your partner is doing it their way...let them!

61. Make individual choices.

62. Your partner has a right to personal choice. So do you.

63. Get interested and get involved.

64. Listen and speak the way a friend does.

65. Take time to be a good friend.

66. Greater communication creates greater intimacy.

67. Stimulate your relationship I.Q.

68. Break out creative juices.

69. Make a commitment to each other to stay together in love.

NOTES

NOTES

NOTES

NOTES

NOTES

BOOT CAMP FOR LOVERS
Nhà xuất bản Thế Giới
46 Trần Hưng Đạo - Hà Nội - Việt Nam

Chịu trách nhiệm xuất bản: Trần Đoàn Lâm
Biên tập: Đông Vĩnh
Trình bày: Smith & Jones
In 500 bản, khổ 15x23cm tại Công ty Cổ phần phát hành sách TP. Hồ Chí
Minh - Việt Nam. Giấy chấp nhận đăng ký kế hoạch xuất bản số 172-
2009/CXB/6-19/ThG, cấp ngày 26/2/2009. In xong và nộp lưu chiểu
tháng 5/2009